GOOFY GOOD CLEAN JOKES

FOR KIDS!

Bob Phillips

Illustrations by
Norm Daniels

HARVEST HOUSE PUBLISHERS
Eugene, Oregon 97402

GOOFY GOOD CLEAN JOKES FOR KIDS!

Copyright © 1994 by Harvest House Publishers
Eugene, Oregon 97402

Library of Congress Cataloging-in-Publication Data

Phillips, Bob, 1940–
    Goofy good clean jokes for kids! / Bob Phillips.
       p.   m.
    ISBN 1-56507-241-3
    1. Riddles, Juvenile. 2. Wit and humor, Juvenile. [1. Jokes.
2. Riddles.] I. Title.
PN6371.5.P487 1994
398.6—dc20   94-14563
                                                  CIP
                                                  AC

Printed in the United States of America.

94 95 96 97 98 99 00 01 — 10 9 8 7 6 5 4 3 2 1

*To the
great, grand,
and goofy
Griffin family.*

Contents

1

Galloping Goofies

What keeps the moon from falling?
Its beams, of course.

•

What kind of robbery may not be dangerous?
A safe robbery.

•

What does the plumber say to his wife when she talks too
    much?
Pipe down.

•

What kind of fish is the most stupid?
A simple salmon.

•

If you were locked in a cemetery at night, how would you
    get out?
Use a skeleton key.

•

What kind of song do you sing in a car?
A cartoon.

•

When can you see yourself in a place you've never been?
When you look into a mirror.

•

What does a garden say when it laughs?
Hoe, hoe, hoe.

•

What is the last thing you take off before going to bed?
Your feet from the floor.

•

Why do birds fly south for the winter?
Because it's too far to walk.

•

What do they call someone whose opinion differs from
    their own?
A radical.

•

When is it right for you to lie?
When you are in bed.

•

How do sailors identify Long Island?
By the Sound.

•

How can a leopard change his spots?
By moving.

What is it that even the smartest person will always over-
look?
His nose.

•

Who is Ferris?
He is a big wheel at the amusement park.

•

Why does a person who is sick lose his sense of touch?
Because he doesn't feel well.

Gaylord & Gladys Goofy

Gaylord: Who delivers breakfast, lunch, and dinner, and always completes his appointed rounds?
Gladys: Beats me.
Gaylord: The mealman.

•

Gaylord: Why do thermometers go to school?
Gladys: I can't guess.
Gaylord: To earn their degrees.

•

Gaylord: Why couldn't the geometry teacher walk?
Gladys: I have no idea.
Gaylord: He had a sprained angle.

•

Gaylord: What do you get when you cross two insects with a rabbit?
Gladys: I don't know.
Gaylord: Bugs Bunny.

•

Gaylord: What state is a number?
Gladys: I have no clue.
Gaylord: Tenn.

•

Gaylord: What is red, white, and blue, and handy if you
    sneeze?
Gladys: You tell me.
Gaylord: Hanky Doodle Dandy.

•

Gaylord: What is stingy, hates Christmas, and lays eggs?
Gladys: I give up.
Gaylord: Ebenezer Chicken.

•

Gaylord: What is big and yellow and comes in the morn-
    ing to brighten mother's day?
Gladys: Who knows?
Gaylord: The school bus.

•

Gaylord: What would you get if you blew your hair dryer
    down a rabbit hole?
Gladys: My mind is a blank.
Gaylord: Hot, cross bunnies.

•

Gaylord: What do you say to Amillion when he does you a
    good turn?
Gladys: That's a mystery.
Gaylord: Thanks, Amillion.

•

Gaylord: What is gray on the inside and clear on the
   outside?
Gladys: Tell me.
Gaylord: An elephant in a Baggie.

Gaylord: What do you say to a hitchhiking frog?
Gladys: You've got me.
Gaylord: Hop in!

Gaylord: What always speaks the truth but doesn't say a
word?
Gladys: I don't have the foggiest.
Gaylord: A mirror.

•

Gaylord: What do you get when you cross an owl with an
oyster?
Gladys: It's unknown to me.
Gaylord: An animal that drops pearls of wisdom.

Grand Goofies

How does an elephant get in a tree?
He hides in an acorn and waits for a squirrel to carry him up.

•

Where do you find tigers?
It depends on where you leave them.

•

Who shot Mussolini eight times?
Five hundred goofy sharpshooters.

•

How do you make antifreeze?
Hide her nightgown.

•

What is gross stupidity?
One hundred and forty-four goofy people.

•

Where do dead letters go?
To the Ghost Office.

•

How does an artist break up with his girlfriend?
He gives her the brush-off.

He was so slow that they had to show him how the waste-
basket worked the first day on his new job.

•

Where is the best place to find books about trees?
A branch library.

•

How did the jewel thief wake up every morning?
To a burglar alarm.

•

When the May Day parade was still a big deal in Moscow,
    a Westerner noted a phalanx of goofy Soviet econo-
    mists marching between military units.
"Why are the goofy economists marching in ranks with
    the army?" the Westerner asked then-President Leonid
    I. Brezhnev.
"You'd be surprised at the damage they do," said the
    president.

•

Where can you find the finest basements?
On the best-cellar list.

•

First goofy man: I just got a bicycle for my girlfriend.
Second goofy man: How did you get such a good trade?

•

How did the barber get rid of his unwanted rabbits?
He used hare remover.

Goofy Gallery

What would happen if all the goofy people in Chicago jumped into Lake Michigan?
Lake Michigan would end up with a ring around it.

•

Did you hear about the four goofy people in a pickup truck that went into a canal? The two in the front were saved, but the two in back were lost because the tailgate was stuck.

•

How do you mail a boat?
You ship it.

•

What constitutes a traditional goofy seven-course dinner?
A can of sardines and a six-pack of soda pop.

•

How do you fit six elephants in a motorboat?
Put three in the front seat and three in the back seat.

•

One goofy kid in our class dresses terribly. The only things that match on him are his belt size and his IQ.

•

Where do fish go to get a degree?
To tuna-versities.

When my little girl got married, I didn't lose a daughter; I gained a goofy son. He moved in with us.

•

How do you catch an electric eel?
With a lightning rod.

•

When you fill me up, I still look empty. What am I?
A balloon.

•

Did you hear about the goofy man who willed his body to
  science? Science is contesting the will.

•

Man: How many slopes did they have at the ski resort you
  went to?
Woman: Three . . . beginners, intermediate, and call-an-
  ambulance!

5

Gertrude & Gerard Goofy

Gertrude: Who has six legs, wears a coonskin cap, and chirps?
Gerard: Beats me.
Gertrude: Davy Cricket.

•

Gertrude: Why shouldn't you ever give your heart to a tennis player?
Gerard: I can't guess.
Gertrude: Because to him, love means nothing.

•

Gertrude: Why did the teenybopper hold a stone up to her left ear and a hamburger bun up to her right ear?
Gerard: I have no idea.
Gertrude: Because she wanted to hear rock-and-roll.

•

Gertrude: What Arizona city is named for a banner pole?
Gerard: I don't have a clue.
Gertrude: Flagstaff.

•

Gertrude: What is easier to give than to receive?
Gerard: You tell me.
Gertrude: Criticism.

•

Gertrude: What did the tree surgeon say to the diseased dogwood?
Gerard: I give up.
Gertrude: Your bark is worse than your blight.

•

Gertrude: What shoes should you wear when your basement is flooded?
Gerard: Who knows?
Gertrude: Pumps.

•

Gertrude: What singing grasshopper lives in a fireplace?
Gerard: You've got me.
Gertrude: Chimney Cricket.

•

Gertrude: What is a fish's favorite game?
Gerard: My mind is a blank.
Gertrude: Salmon Says.

•

Gertrude: What is a thief's favorite game?
Gerard: That's a mystery.
Gertrude: Hide-n-sneak.

•

Gertrude: What family car doesn't move?
Gerard: Tell me.
Gertrude: A stationary wagon.

Gertrude: What did the chewing gum say to the shoe?
Gerard: I don't know.
Gertrude: I'm stuck on you.

Gertrude: What do frogs drink at snack time?
Gerard: I don't have the foggiest.
Gertrude: Croak-a-Cola.

•

Gertrude: What kind of geese are found in Portugal?
Gerard: It's unknown to me.
Gertrude: Portu-geese.

6

Goofy students

First student: The teacher gave me an F-minus.
Second student: Why did she do that?
First student: She says I not only didn't learn anything this year, but I probably forgot most of the stuff I learned last year as well.

•

Teacher: Mrs. Grey, your son is a constant troublemaker. How do you put up with him?

Mrs. Grey: I can't. That's why I send him to school.

•

Teacher: What, besides a supersonic jet, goes faster than the speed of sound?

Student: My Aunt Gladys when she talks.

•

Teacher: When was the Great Depression?

Student: Last week when I got my report card.

•

Teacher: What is a leading cause of dry skin?

Student: Towels.

•

Teacher: Can you name two responsibilities you have at home?

Student: Get out, and stay out.

7

Gooney Goofies

What kind of goofy waiter never accepts tips?
A dumb waiter.

•

What is the difference between a cat and a match?
The cat lights on its feet, and the match lights on its head.

•

How many Californians does it take to change a light bulb?
None. Californians don't put in light bulbs; they put in hot tubs.

•

What is it that you can't hold for five minutes yet is as light as a feather?
Your breath.

•

What headlines do women like least?
Wrinkles.

•

What do you call a lady letter carrier?
A mail female.

●

Why can't the world ever come to an end?
Because it's round.

What happens when the human body is completely submerged in water?
The telephone rings.

●

How can you tell if a student is hungry?
When he devours books.

●

How do you play Russian roulette in India?
You play the flute with six cobras around you, and one of them is deaf.

•

Is Ballpoint really the name of your pig?
No, that's just his pen name.

•

Who was the greatest Irish inventor?
Pat Pending.

•

What happened when two geese had a head-on collision?
They got goose bumps.

•

What do you call a 30-pound book when you use it as a weapon?
A book club.

•

How does your stamp album feel when it's kept in the refrigerator?
Cool, calm, and collected.

•

Which is faster: hot or cold?
Hot is faster. You can catch cold.

Gustave & Gilberta
Goofy

Gustave: Who is white, has two eyes made out of coal, and can't move fast?
Gilberta: Beats me.
Gustave: Frosty the Slowman.

•

Gustave: Why is it bad to write a letter on an empty stomach?
Gilberta: I can't guess.
Gustave: Because it's much better to write on paper.

•

Gustave: Why was the 2,000-year-old flower wrapped in strips of cloth?
Gilberta: I have no idea.
Gustave: It was a chrysanthemummy.

•

Gustave: What belongs to you, but is used more often by others?
Gilberta: I don't have a clue.
Gustave: Your name.

•

Gustave: What do you do if you smash your toe?
Gilberta: You tell me.
Gustave: You call a toe truck.

Gustave: What is the best thing to put in a pie?
Gilberta: I don't know.
Gustave: Your teeth.

Gustave: What changes color every two seconds?
Gilberta: I give up.
Gustave: A chameleon with the hiccups.

Gustave: What happens when an ear of corn gets dandruff?
Gilberta: Who knows?
Gustave: It ends up with corn flakes.

•

Gustave: What does the sneezing champion of the Olympics win?
Gilberta: You've got me.
Gustave: A cold medal.

•

Gustave: What is worse than being with a fool?
Gilberta: My mind is a blank.
Gustave: Fooling with a bee.

•

Gustave: What kind of bee drops its honey?
Gilberta: That's a mystery.
Gustave: A spilling bee.

•

Gustave: What is the difference between a barber and a woman with many children?
Gilberta: Tell me.
Gustave: One has razors to shave, the other has shavers to raise.

•

Gustave: What squawks and jumps out of airplanes?
Gilberta: I don't have the foggiest.
Gustave: A parrot-trooper.

•

Gustave: What do attorneys wear to work?
Gilberta: It's unknown to me.
Gustave: Lawsuits.

9

Goofy Definitions

Amount: What a soldier in the cavalry rides.

•

Antiques: Merchandise sold for old times' sake.

•

Appeal: What a banana comes in.

•

Boycott: A bed for a small male child.

•

Beastly weather: Raining cats and dogs.

•

Carpet: A cat or dog who enjoys riding in an automobile.

•

Circle: A round straight line with a hole in the middle.

•

Compliment: The applause that refreshes.

•

Endangered species: A kid who gets straight F's on his report card.

•

Falsehood: Someone who pretends to be a gangster.

•

Fodder: The man who married mudder.

•

Gruesome: A little taller than before.

•

Half-wit: A person who spends half of his time thinking up wisecracks and goofy definitions.

•

Knapsack: A sleeping bag.

•

Map: Something that will tell you everything except how to fold it up again.

•

Pedestrian: A father who has kids who can drive.

•

Stork: The bird with the big bill.

•

Screen door: What kids get a bang out of.

•

Ventriloquist: A person who talks to himself for a living.

•

Turtle: A reptile who lives in a mobile home.

Goofy Doctors

Patient: Don't you think I should get a second opinion?
Doctor: Sure. Come back tomorrow.

•

Patient: What would you take for this cold?
Doctor: Make me an offer.

•

Patient: Am I going to die?
Doctor: That's the last thing you're going to do.

•

Wife: Thank you so much for making this house call to see my husband.
Doctor: Think nothing of it. There is another man in the neighborhood who is sick, and I thought I could kill two birds with one stone.

•

Patient: Am I getting better?
Doctor: I don't know. Let me feel your purse.

•

Patient: Should I file my nails?
Doctor: No. Throw them away like everybody else.

•

Patient: How can I avoid falling hair?
Doctor: Step to one side.

Patient: You're charging me ten dollars and all you did
   was paint my throat.
Doctor: What did you expect for ten dollars—wallpaper?

•

Patient: What should I do if my temperature goes up
   another point?
Doctor: Sell!

•

You tell 'em Doctor. You've got the patience.

•

Patient: How long will I live?
Doctor: You should live to be 80.
Patient: I *am* 80.
Doctor: What did I tell you?

•

Patient: My hair is coming out. What can you give me to
   keep it in?
Doctor: A cigar box.

Goofies Galore

Which burns longer: a white candle or a black one?
Neither. Both burn shorter.

•

If you were invited out to dinner and saw nothing but a
   beet on your plate, what would you say?
"That beet's all!"

•

Which key is the hardest to turn?
A donkey.

•

In what month do girls talk the least?
February, because it is the shortest.

•

Which bird can lift the most weight?
The crane.

•

Who was the world's greatest glutton?
A man who bolted a door, threw up a window, then sat down and swallowed a whole story.

When the clock strikes 13, what time is it?
Time to get the clock fixed.

•

How many evolutionists does it take to change a light bulb?
Only one, but it takes him eight million years.

•

How would you define the daffodil?
A goofy pickle.

●

What do they call a towel that you look at but never use?
A guest towel.

●

What two flowers grow best in a zoo?
Dandelions and tiger lilies.

●

When is an elevator not an elevator?
When it is going down.

●

Why are telephone rates so high in Iran?
Because everyone speaks Persian-to-Persian.

●

What cord is full of knots that no one can untie?
A cord of wood.

●

Why is a kiss like gossip?
Because it goes from mouth to mouth.

Geneva & Guthrie
Goofy

Geneva: Who rides in a sleigh, gives Christmas presents, and has many faults?
Guthrie: Beats me.
Geneva: Santa Flaws.

•

Geneva: Why should men avoid the letter *a*?
Guthrie: I can't guess.
Geneva: Because it makes men mean.

•

Geneva: Why does Uncle Sam wear red, white, and blue suspenders?
Guthrie: I have no idea.
Geneva: To hold up his pants.

•

Geneva: What does a worm do in a cornfield?
Guthrie: I don't have a clue.
Geneva: It goes in one ear and out the other.

•

Geneva: What animal is satisfied with the least nourish-
ment?
Guthrie: You tell me.
Geneva: Moths. They eat nothing but holes.

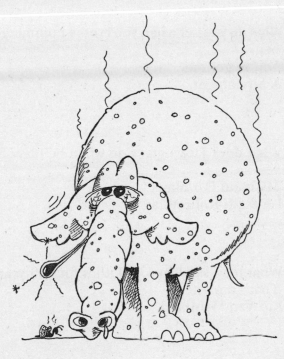

Geneva: What has spots, weighs four tons, and loves
peanuts?
Guthrie: I don't know.
Geneva: An elephant with the measles.

•

Geneva: What do you call a carrot who insults a farmer?
Guthrie: I give up.
Geneva: A fresh vegetable.

•

Geneva: What has one eye, one horn, and flies?
Guthrie: Who knows?
Geneva: A half-blind rhinoceros in an airplane.

•

Geneva: What do you get when you cross a hummingbird
with a bell?
Guthrie: You've got me.
Geneva: A humdinger.

•

Geneva: What does Jack's giant do when he plays foot-
ball?
Guthrie: My mind is a blank.
Geneva: He fee-fi-fo-fumbles.

•

Geneva: What man slept in his clothes for 100 years?
Guthrie: That's a mystery.
Geneva: Rip Van Wrinkled.

•

Geneva: What do whales do when they feel sad?
Guthrie: Tell me.
Geneva: Blubber.

•

Geneva: What kind of soda can't you drink?
Guthrie: I don't have the foggiest.
Geneva: Baking soda.

•

Geneva: What kinds of toys does a psychiatrist's child play with?
Guthrie: It's unknown to me.
Geneva: Mental blocks.

•

Geneva: What two garden vegetables fight crime?
Guthrie: I'm in the dark.
Geneva: Beetman and Radish.

•

Geneva: What kind of ties can't you wear?
Guthrie: Search me.
Geneva: Railroad ties.

Great Goofies

How did the rocket lose his job?
He was fired.

•

How long is a Chinaman?
Of course! (How Long is his name.)

•

Why did the goofy boy take a hammer to bed with him?
He wanted to hit the sack.

•

Where is the best place to have a broken bone?
On someone else.

•

What is worse than raining cats and dogs?
Hailing taxis and buses.

•

What did Paul Revere say when he finished his famous
  ride?
Whoa!

•

Why does a dog wag his tail?
Because he wants to.

•

What should you do when your sister falls asleep in
  church?
Polka.

•

Where is the capital of the United States?
All over the world.

•

What is always coming but never arrives?
Tomorrow.

•

How do you spell Mississippi with one eye?
Close one eye and spell it.

•

What do you get when a bird flies into a fan?
Shredded tweet.

•

Which is correct: The yolk of an egg *is* white? Or the
  yolks of eggs *are* white?
Neither. The yolk of an egg is yellow.

•

What would a home be without children?
Quiet.

Why did the goofy farmer put the cow on the scale?
He wanted to see how much the milky weighed.

14

Giggling Goofies

What do you call a formal dance for butchers?
A meatball.

•

If you see the handwriting on the wall, there's a child in
the family.

•

I come from a broken home. My kids have broken everything in it.

•

We have a kid in our class who dresses like a million
bucks. Everything he wears is all wrinkled and green.

•

It takes 12 one-cent stamps to make a dozen. How many
six-cent stamps does it take to make a dozen?
*It takes 12 of anything to make a dozen—even six-cent
stamps.*

•

First teacher: Gene got a zero on the test today.
Second teacher: That's nothing.

•

First man: For the last ten years my mother-in-law has been living with my wife and me in the same apartment.
Second man: So, why don't you tell her to get out?
First man: I can't. It's her apartment.

•

There's too much violence on TV these days. The other day I saw two murders, six fights, an earthquake, and a nuclear disaster. That's the last time I'll watch the Saturday morning cartoons.

•

Gina: My dog has a sweet tooth.
Gabe: How do you know that?
Gina: He only chases bakery trucks.

•

Gerald: I'm giving my girlfriend a striking and timely present for her birthday.
Garth: What did you get her?
Gerald: An alarm clock.

•

I once ate in a goofy restaurant that was so bad I got food poisoning just from opening the menu.

•

How do you crush an orange?
Tell it you don't love it anymore.

•

Life on other planets must be intelligent. So far, they have had enough sense not to establish diplomatic relations with earth.

The food in our school cafeteria is so bad that last night they caught a mouse trying to phone out for pizza.

•

Gloria: Did you hear about the head of cabbage, the hose, and the bottle of ketchup that were having a race?
Gretta: No, how did it go?
Gloria: The cabbage was ahead, the hose was still running, and the bottle of ketchup was trying to catch up.

•

They call him King Chicken. He's the biggest cluck in town.

•

Griff: Have you heard the joke about the big burp?
Gretchen: No.
Griff: Never mind, it's not worth repeating.

•

What nasty bug is responsible for eating up the poor farmer's cotton?
The evil weevil.

•

You tell 'em, banana. You've been skinned.

•

You tell 'em, aviator. You're a high flyer.

•

You tell 'em, operator. You've got their number.

•

Where do they send homeless dogs?
To an arf-anage.

15

Grover & Gretchen
Goofy

Grover: Why did the rich lady buy a Ming vase?
Gretchen: I can't guess.
Grover: To go with her Ming coat.

•

Grover: Why do elephants have ivory tusks?
Gretchen: I have no idea.
Grover: Iron tusks would rust.

•

Grover: Why would a man in jail want to catch the measles?
Gretchen: I don't know.
Grover: So he could break out.

•

Grover: What bone can't a dog eat?
Gretchen: You tell me.
Grover: A trombone.

•

Grover: What do you get when you trip an elephant carrying a crate of oranges?
Gretchen: I give up.
Grover: Orange juice.

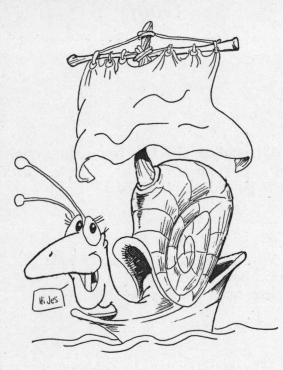

Grover: What is the world's slowest ship?
Gretchen: Tell me.
Grover: A snailboat.

•

Grover: What is another name for a cowboy?
Gretchen: Who knows?
Grover: A bull.

•

Grover: What kind of bird eats the same worm eight times?
Gretchen: You've got me.
Grover: A swallow with the hiccups.

•

Grover: What do you do if there's a kidnapping in Texas?
Gretchen: My mind is a blank.
Grover: Wake him up.

•

Grover: What does Mickey Mouse's girlfriend wear?
Gretchen: That's a mystery.
Grover: Minnie skirts.

•

Grover: What do you get when you cross a skunk with a raccoon?
Gretchen: I don't have the foggiest.
Grover: A dirty look from the raccoon.

•

Grover: What happens when you ask an oyster a personal question?
Gretchen: It's unknown to me.
Grover: It clams up.

•

Grover: What has wings, is out of its mind, and sits in trees?
Gretchen: I'm in the dark.
Grover: A raven lunatic.

Genuinely Goofy

What steps should you take if a tiger charges you?
Long ones.

•

What did the judge say when the skunk came into the
    courtroom?
Odor in the court!

•

When is a black dog not a black dog?
When he is a greyhound.

•

What is the difference between a hungry person and a
    greedy person?
One longs to eat, and the other eats too long.

•

What is smaller than an ant's mouth?
An ant's dinner.

•

What is the surest way to double your money?
Fold it.

●

Why is a sleeping baby like a hijacking?
Because it's a kid napping.

Do you know why the cow jumped over the moon?
The farmer had cold hands.

●

How can you tell if there is an elephant under your bed?
The ceiling is very close.

•

What is a diploma?
Da man who fixa da pipes when dey leak.

•

What is the difference between kissing your sister and
    kissing your sweetheart?
About 25 seconds.

•

How do you stop a charging lion?
Take away his credit cards.

•

What is the difference between a tuna fish and a piano?
You can't tune a fish.

•

What is deaf, dumb, and blind and always tells the truth?
A mirror.

Goofy Knock-Knocks

Knock, knock.
Who's there?
Osborn.
Osborn who?
Osborn in August.

•

Knock, knock.
Who's there?
Max.
Max who?
Max no difference. Let me in.

•

Knock, knock.
Who's there?
Kleenex.
Kleenex who?
Kleenex are prettier than dirty necks.

•

Knock, knock.
Who's there?
Adore.
Adore who?
Adore is between us. Open up!

Knock, knock.
Who's there?
Hewlett.
Hewlett who?
Hewlett the cat out of the bag?

Knock, knock.
Who's there?
Eyewash.
Eyewash who?
Eyewash I had a million dollars.

•

Knock, knock.
Who's there?
Stan.
Stan who?
Stan back! I'm coming in.

•

Knock, knock.
Who's there?
Allacin.
Allacin who?
Allacin Wonderland.

•

Knock, knock.
Who's there?
Dewey.
Dewey who?
Dewey have to listen to all this knocking?

•

Knock, knock.
Who's there?
Wooden.
Wooden who?
Wooden you like to go out with me?

•

Knock, knock.
Who's there?
Adele.
Adele who?
Adele is where the farmer's in.

•

Knock, knock.
Who's there?
Caesar.
Caesar who?
Caesar jolly good fellow, Caesar jolly good fellow.

•

Knock, knock.
Who's there?
Thatcher.
Thatcher who?
Thatcher was a funny joke.

•

Knock, knock.
Who's there?
Boo-hoo.
Boo-hoo who?
Boo-hoo-hoo.
Boo-hoo-hoo who?
Boo-hoo-hoo-hoo.
Boo-hoo-hoo-hoo who?
Boo-hoo-hoo-hoo-hoo.
Boo-hoo-hoo-hoo-hoo who?
Stop it! You're breaking my heart.

•

Knock, knock.
Who's there?
Jupiter.
Jupiter who?
Jupiter fly in my soup?

•

Knock, knock.
Who's there?
Amaryllis.
Amaryllis who?
Amaryllis state agent. Wanna buy a house?

•

Knock, Knock.
Who's there?
Popeye.
Popeye who?
Popeye've got to have the car tonight.

•

Knock, knock.
Who's there?
Hi, this is just Diane.
Just Diane who?
Just Diane to see you.

Gwendolyn & Godfrey Goofy

Gwendolyn: Who carries a basket, visits grandma, and steals jewelry?
Godfrey: Beats me.
Gwendolyn: Little Red Robbin' Hood.

•

Gwendolyn: Why is it hard to drive a golf ball?
Godfrey: I have no idea.
Gwendolyn: Because it doesn't have a steering wheel.

•

Gwendolyn: What cereal goes snap, crackle, squeak?
Godfrey: I don't know.
Gwendolyn: Mice Krispies.

•

Gwendolyn: What did the parrot say to the streetcar?
Godfrey: I don't have a clue.
Gwendolyn: Trolley want a cracker?

•

Gwendolyn: What has big eyes, green skin, and lives alone?
Godfrey: I give up.
Gwendolyn: Hermit the Frog.

•

Gwendolyn: What is big and white and scores a lot of strikes?
Godfrey: Who knows?
Gwendolyn: A bowler bear.

•

Gwendolyn: What does Sherlock Holmes read for fun?
Godfrey: You've got me.
Gwendolyn: The ency-clue-pedia.

•

Gwendolyn: What do you get when you cross the United States and the United Kingdom?
Godfrey: My mind is a blank.
Gwendolyn: The Atlantic Ocean.

•

Gwendolyn: What time is it when the kids need a nap?
Godfrey: Tell me.
Gwendolyn: Whine o'clock.

•

Gwendolyn: What does Sleeping Beauty gargle with?
Godfrey: I don't have the foggiest.
Gwendolyn: Rinse Charming.

•

Gwendolyn: What do you call a formal dance for turkeys?
Godfrey: It's unknown to me.
Gwendolyn: A turkey trot.

Gwendolyn: Why was the baseball player asked to come along on the camping trip?
Godfrey: I can't guess.
Gwendolyn: They needed someone to pitch the tent.

Gwendolyn: What do you get when you cross bubble gum, a hen, and a dog?
Godfrey: You tell me.
Gwendolyn: Snap, cackle, and pup.

•

Gwendolyn: What did Mr. Bird call his son?
Godfrey: I'm in the dark.
Gwendolyn: A chirp off the old block.

Going Goofy

Stuffy singer: I sing with the voice of a bird.
Listener: I know—a crow.

•

I never tell jokes about ceilings because the punch lines
   always go over everyone's heads.

•

When you order bison steaks at a restaurant, what does
   the waiter bring you after the meal?
A Buffalo Bill.

•

Glenn: Did you hear about the wall that turned to a life of
   crime?
Gwen: No. What did he do?
Glenn: He went around holding up ceilings.

•

You tell 'em, horse. You carry a tale.

•

If in a restaurant you must choose between eating an
  elephant egg or a 500-pound canary egg, which
  should you choose?
*A 500-pound canary egg, because everyone hates elephant
  yolks.*

We just heard that Italy is sponsoring a new award for
  excellence in the art of cooking pizza. It's called the
  Nobel Pizza Prize.

•

A catty remark often has more lives than a cat.

•

First man: That's a beautiful stuffed tiger you've got
  there. Where did you get him?
Second man: In India, when I was on a hunting expedi-
  tion with my uncle.
First man: What is he stuffed with?
Second man: My uncle.

•

First kid: Did you know that Daniel Boone's brothers
  were all famous doctors?
Second kid: No way.
First kid: Don't tell me you never heard of the Boone
  Docs?

•

I'm not as stupid as I look. Last week a wise guy tried to
  sell me the Statue of Liberty and I didn't give him any
  money—until he gave me a ten-year guarantee on the
  flame.

•

Did you ever hear of Amoeba State Prison? It's so small it
  has only one cell.

•

My father taught me how to swim when I was five years
  old. He took me down to the river and threw me in. I
  wouldn't have minded, but people were ice skating at
  the time.

•

Scientist: Do you know what will happen when man
  pollutes outer space?
Man: Yes. The Milky Way will curdle.

•

I think our currency is headed for another fall on the world market. Yesterday, I looked at a five-dollar bill and Abraham Lincoln was wearing a crash helmet.

•

Man: I got airsick again last week.
Woman: Oh, were you in an airplane?
Man: No, in Los Angeles.

•

In a bakery window: *Pie like mother used to buy.*

•

Two frogs were sitting on a lily pad. One leaned over to the other and said, "Time sure is fun when you're having flies."

•

First kid: Hey, I have an idea!
Second kid: Beginner's luck.

•

You tell 'em, clock. You've got the time.

Giddy Goofies

I got straight F's in the sixth grade this year. That is not good, but it is a slight improvement over what I did in the sixth grade last year.

•

When do Eskimo travel in heavy traffic?
At mush hour.

•

Where do sheep go when they want to barter?
To the five-and-ten because they know they will get their Woolworth.

•

What do you have when you extend your little finger?
A goofy handkerchief.

•

When does a horse talk?
Whinny wants to.

•

How do you spell pickle backwards?
P-I-C-K-L-E B-A-C-K-W-A-R-D-S.

•

Where do bacteria go on vacation?
Germany.

I had one friend who was a real dummy. He lost his shoes
one time because he put them on the wrong feet. Then
he couldn't remember whose feet he put them on.

•

Then there was the goofy man who put on one boot because the weather forecaster said there would be only one foot of snow.

•

How do you spell blind pig in six letters?
B-L-N-D P-G.

•

Where do you buy laundry detergent?
In a soapermarket.

•

Her luck was so bad that her contacts got cataracts.

•

How do army frogs march?
Hop, two, three, four!

Gideon & Gloria Goofy

Gideon: Who does Clark Kent turn into when he is hungry?
Gloria: Beats me.
Gideon: Supperman.

•

Gideon: Why did the farmer get a ticket?
Gloria: I can't guess.
Gideon: He exceeded the seed limit.

•

Gideon: Why did the swimmer get a ticket?
Gloria: I have no idea.
Gideon: He was caught diving without a license.

•

Gideon: What big cat lives in people's backyards?
Gloria: I don't have a clue.
Gideon: A clothes lion.

•

Gideon: What happened when the cat swallowed a ball of
yarn?
Gloria: You tell me.
Gideon: She had mittens.

Gideon: What dog do you find at the United Nations?
Gloria: I don't know.
Gideon: A diplo-mutt.

•

Gideon: What is a minister doing when he rehearses his
sermon?
Gloria: I give up.
Gideon: Practicing what he preaches.

•

Gideon: What do you call the boss at a dairy?
Gloria: Who knows?
Gideon: The big cheese.

•

Gideon: What do you call it when five toads sit on top of each other?
Gloria: You've got me.
Gideon: A toad-em pole.

•

Gideon: What music do steelworkers play at their parties?
Gloria: My mind is a blank.
Gideon: Heavy metal.

•

Gideon: What university do dogs go to?
Gloria: That's a mystery.
Gideon: Bark-ley.

•

Gideon: What is a mouse's favorite game?
Gloria: Tell me.
Gideon: Hide-n-squeak.

•

Gideon: What do you get if you tie two bicycles together?
Gloria: I don't have the foggiest.
Gideon: Siamese Schwinns.

•

Gideon: What is the funniest car on the road?
Gloria: It's unknown to me.
Gideon: A Jolkswagen.

Golden Goofies

Who was the first man to make a monkey of himself?
Darwin.

•

What are the largest ants in the world?
Elephants.

•

What do they call someone who can stick to a reducing diet?
A good loser.

•

How far is it from one end of the earth to the other?
A day's journey.

•

What is the best part about owning tiny TV sets?
Tiny commercials.

•

Why do we all go to bed?
Because the bed will not come to us.

What increases in value by half when you turn it upside
down?
The number 6.

What time is it when an elephant sits on your fence?
Time to buy a new fence.

When does a boat show affection?
When it hugs the shore.

What does 36 inches make in Glasgow?
One Scotland Yard.

●

Why can't it rain for two days in a row?
Because there is always a night in between.

●

Why is a bank robbery like a pair of suspenders?
Because they are both holdups.

●

What is the best way to make time go by fast?
Use the spur of the moment.

●

What kinds of animals can jump higher than the Statue
of Liberty?
Any kind. The Statue of Liberty can't jump.

●

Why do we dress girl babies in pink and boy babies in
blue?
Because they can't dress themselves.

Goofy Gags

What did one tail pipe say to the other tail pipe?
I'm exhausted.

•

Why does electricity shock people?
Because it doesn't know how to conduct itself.

•

Who can stay single even if he marries many women?
A minister.

•

What has a heart in its head?
Lettuce.

•

If you were dying and you had only a dime, what would
you buy?
A pack of Lifesavers.

•

What do you need to know to teach tricks to a grasshopper?
More than the grasshopper.

•

When is it proper to refer to a person as a pig?
When he is a boar.

What is the best way to paint a rabbit?
With hare spray.

•

How do you make a Big Mac monster burger?
You put two people patties, special sauce, lettuce, cheese, pickles, and onions on a sesame seed bun.

•

What animal doesn't play fair?
The cheetah.

•

What will stay hot the longest in the refrigerator?
Red pepper.

•

What word do most people like best?
The last.

•

Why did the traffic light turn red?
If you had to change in front of all those people, you would turn red, too.

•

What happens when a chimpanzee twists his ankle?
He gets a monkey wrench.

•

What pen is never used for writing?
A pigpen.

Geraldine & Gaspar
Goofy

Geraldine: Who are the most despised football players?
Gaspar: Beats me.
Geraldine: The offensive team.

•

Geraldine: Why do golfers wear two pairs of pants?
Gaspar: I can't guess.
Geraldine: In case they get a hole in one.

•

Geraldine: Why do lions roar?
Gaspar: I have no idea.
Geraldine: They would feel silly saying oink, oink.

•

Geraldine: What amusement-park ride is only 12 inches long?
Gaspar: I don't know.
Geraldine: A ruler coaster.

•

Geraldine: What does a student need if he is absent from school during final exams?
Gaspar: You tell me.
Geraldine: A good excuse.

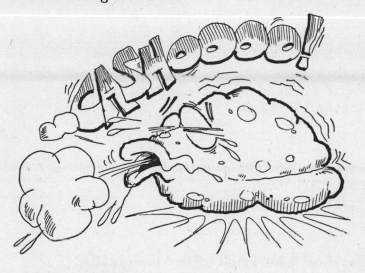

Geraldine: What nut is like a sneeze?
Gaspar: I don't have a clue.
Geraldine: A cashew.

•

Geraldine: What vitamin has good vision?
Gaspar: I give up.
Geraldine: Vitamin C.

•

Geraldine: What do you get when you cross an elephant with a Volkswagen?
Gaspar: Who knows?
Geraldine: A little car with a big trunk.

•

Geraldine: What did the silly comedian bake on his day off?
Gaspar: You've got me.
Geraldine: Corn bread.

•

Geraldine: What do you get when you cross a stream and a brook?
Gaspar: My mind is a blank.
Geraldine: Wet feet.

•

Geraldine: What do magicians say on Halloween?
Gaspar: Tell me.
Geraldine: Trick or trick?

•

Geraldine: What kind of lizard loves riddles?
Gaspar: I don't have the foggiest.
Geraldine: A sillymander.

•

Geraldine: What is the strangest kind of commercial?
Gaspar: It's unknown to me.
Geraldine: An oddvertisement.

Good-Humored Goofies

Where can you always find happiness?
In the dictionary.

•

How do you make a slow employee fast?
Don't give him anything to eat for a while.

•

What is worse than a centipede with corns?
A hippopotamus with chapped lips.

•

What adds color and flavor to a very popular pastime?
Lipstick.

•

Why did the comedian's wife sue for divorce?
She claimed he was trying to joke her to death.

•

What is the center of gravity?
V.

•

What kind of lights did Noah have on his ark?
Floodlights.

•

What animal drops from the clouds?
The rain, dear.

What do you call a nut that never remembers?
A forget-me-nut.

•

Why should you borrow money from a pessimist?
Because he never expects to get it back.

•

If you threw a green shoe into the Red Sea, what would it become?
Wet.

•

What is the name of the saddest bird alive?
The bluebird.

•

How many hamburgers can you eat on an empty stomach?
Only one, because after that your stomach is no longer empty.

•

What sits up with a woman when her husband is out late?
Her imagination.

•

What can you make by putting two banana peels together?
A pair of slippers.

Goofy Goodies

You can't convince me crime doesn't pay. Last week I was standing on a curb and a limousine pulled up in front of me. A chauffeur got out, rolled out a red carpet, and opened the back door for a mugger who robbed me.

•

In a Maine classroom, Miss Hubbard was telling her pupils how people from different states are given nicknames based on something of significance about their state.

"For example," she explained, "people from North Carolina are called 'Tarheels,' people from Ohio are called 'buckeyes,' and those from Indiana are called 'Hoosiers.' Now, can any of you tell me what they call people from our state of Maine?"

Arlene raised her hand. "Maniacs!"

•

Have you ever seen a horse fly?

•

Have you ever seen an egg box?

•

Garth: I'm going to have to let that new secretary go.
Gertha: Don't you think he is learning word processing fast enough?
Garth: I don't think so. There is too much White-Out on the monitor screen!

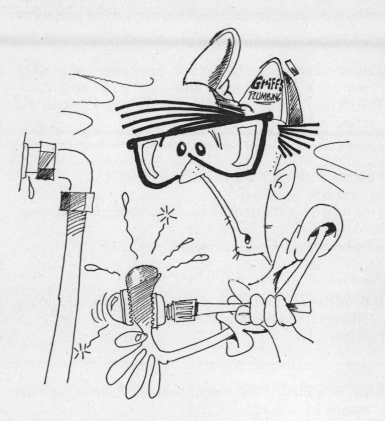

If a gardener has a green thumb, who has a purple thumb?
A nearsighted plumber.

Ranch visitor: This is the biggest ranch I have ever seen. How many head of cattle have you got over there?
Goofy rancher: Can't tell. They are facing the wrong way.

•

The trouble with dark-horse candidates is you can't find out about their track record until you are saddled with them.

•

Talk about being dumb. A robber jumped out of an alley, pointed a gun at a man, and said, "Give me $50."
The victim replied, "I'm sorry, I don't have $50. Can you break a $100 bill?"

•

First boy: My cat ate a whole ball of wool.
Second boy: So what?
First boy: So her kittens were all born wearing sweaters.
Second boy: That's some yarn.
First boy: Well, I'm a knit-wit.

•

If dentists pull out police officers' teeth, what do police officers do to dentists' teeth?
Pull them over.

•

I live in a high-crime neighborhood. Even our police station has a burglar alarm.

•

Goofy bachelor: Listen, baby, you have to admit that guys like me don't grow on trees.
Girl: No, they swing from them!

•

Buyer: Hey, you told me you had purebred police dogs for sale. This animal is the mangiest, dirtiest, scrawniest mutt I have ever laid my eyes on! How can you get away with calling him a police dog?
Breeder: He works undercover.

•

Greg: How was your trip to Helsinki?
Gean: Terrible! All our luggage vanished into Finn Air!

•

Lady: What a cute little boy! What is your name, sweetheart?
Little boy: Connor.
Lady: Can you tell me your full name?
Little boy: Connor Stop That!

•

Gwin: Well, excuse me for living!
Gilbert: OK, but don't let it happen again.

•

First man (reading statistics from a newspaper): Do you know that every time I breathe, someone dies?
Second man: Have you tried using mouthwash?

•

In a car wash: Grime does not pay.

•

You tell 'em, cashier. I'm a poor teller.

•

You tell 'em, hunter. I'm game.

•

You tell 'em, Simon. I'll agree.

•

"My business is down in the dumps," said the goofy garbage man.

•

Five-year-old Bobby sat on the front porch holding his cat. A little girl who lived around the corner approached him and said, "What is your cat's name?"
"Ben Hur," replied the little boy.
"How did you happen to call it that?"
"We used to call it Ben—until it had kittens."

Gus & Gabriel Goofy

Gus: Who is the nastiest Disney character?
Gabriel: Beats me.
Gus: Meanie Mouse.

•

Gus: Why did the paintbrush retire?
Gabriel: I can't guess.
Gus: It had a stroke.

•

Gus: What do you get when you cross a dog with a chicken?
Gabriel: I don't know.
Gus: A pooched egg.

•

Gus: What do you get when you cross a cat with a lemon?
Gabriel: I don't have a clue.
Gus: A sour puss.

•

Gus: What kind of music can you play with a shoehorn?
Gabriel: I give up.
Gus: Footnotes.

Gus: Why did the umpire throw the chicken out of the baseball game?
Gabriel: I have no idea.
Gus: He suspected fowl play.

Gus: What is a liar's favorite month?
Gabriel: Who knows?
Gus: Fib-ruary.

•

Gus: What kind of shot do you give a sick car?
Gabriel: You've got me.
Gus: A fuel injection.

•

Gus: What does the government use when it takes a
census of all the monkeys in the zoos?
Gabriel: My mind is a blank.
Gus: An ape recorder.

•

Gus: What are the last three hairs on a dog's tail called?
Gabriel: That's a mystery.
Gus: Dog hairs.

•

Gus: What is black and white and has sixteen wheels?
Gabriel: Tell me.
Gus: A zebra on roller skates.

•

Gus: What do you get when you cross a watchdog with a
wolf?
Gabriel: I don't have the foggiest.
Gus: A very nervous mailman.

Gadzooks...
More Goofies!

Greta: I always get sick the night before I take a trip.
Greg: Then why don't you leave a day earlier?

•

Gene: Did you hear about the guy from Rome who wanted to swim the English Channel but couldn't?
Geanie: No, what about him?
Gene: He could only swim in Italian.

•

Gretchen: An apple a day keeps the doctor away.
Gabe: What keeps the friends away?
Gretchen: Bad breath.

•

Mr. Green: Why, when I first came to this city, I was jobless, penniless, shoeless, and without a shred of clothing!
Interviewer: You mean...
Mr. Green: That's right! I was born here!

•

Georgina: Did you hear about the terrible accident? A pink cruise ship collided with a purple cruise ship.
George: What happened?
Georgina: All the passengers were marooned!

•

Gwen: So, you are expecting your seventh child! What do you think you'll call it?
Gina: I think I'll call it quits!

•

My husband has a one-track mind . . . and it's the slow lane.

•

Customer: Are 500-pound canaries intelligent?
Shopkeeper: Of course not. They're all birdbrains.

•

Crooks are becoming bolder than ever. The last time I was robbed, the mugger gave me his card in case I was ever in the neighborhood again.

•

Rumor has it that a boxer who gets beat up in a fight is usually a sore loser.

•

A little boy showed his teacher his drawing, entitled "America the Beautiful." In the center was an airplane covered with apples, pears, oranges, and bananas.
"What is this?" the teacher asked, pointing to the airplane.
"That," answered the boy, "is the fruited plane."

•

The only thing I know about my husband's family tree is that monkeys once lived in it.

Gerald: What is flat at the bottom, pointed at the top, and has ears?
Gene: I give up.
Gerald: A mountain.
Gene: Oh yeah? What about the ears?
Gerald: Haven't you ever heard of mountaineers?

•

Griff: My Uncle Guy is running for mayor.
Gretta: Honest?
Griff: No, but that's not stopping him.

•

We had a food fight in the school cafeteria today. The food won.

•

Guy: Every morning I dream I'm falling from a 10-story building and just before I hit the ground, I wake up.

Grace: That's terrible. What are you going to do about it?

Guy: I'm going to move into a 15-story building. I need more sleep.

•

Geoffe: Did you know there was a kidnapping down the street?

Geaney: No, what happened?

Geoffe: His mother woke him up.

•

The doctor called Griff to let him know the results of his physical exam. "Griff, I've got bad news and worse news. The bad news is that you have 24 hours to live."

"Oh, no," said Griff. "That's bad, but what could possibly be worse than that?"

"I've been trying to get you since yesterday," said the doctor.

•

A man suffering from terrible headaches goes to his doctor.

"Your brain is diseased," said the doctor.

"What can you do to help me?" asked the man.

"The only possibility is a new brain transplant. But the problem is that brains are not covered by medical insurance."

"Doc, I have some money; what will it cost me?"

"Depends on the donor," said the doctor. "A secretary's brain will cost you about $35,000, and an executive's brain will set you back close to $250,000."

"Wait a second," said the patient. "The difference between $35,000 and $250,000 is vast. How can you justify such an incredible discrepancy?"

"Simple!" said the doctor. "The executive's brain has hardly been used."

•

Old baseball players never have mental breakdowns. They just go a little batty.

•

Did you hear the story about the snake trainers? It was rather charming.

•

The boss was watching his new employee count out the day's receipts and asked the man where he got his financial training.
"Yale," he answered.
"Good. And what is your name?"
"Yackson."

•

Garth: You are calling me an idiot? After 15 years of marriage!
Gracie: You are right. I'm sorry. I shouldn't have waited so long.

•

The meat at lunch today was so tough that half the class was kept after school so we could finish chewing it.

•

First boy: A train just passed.
Second boy: How can you tell?
First boy: I can see its tracks.

Other Books by Bob Phillips

For information on how to purchase any of the above books, contact your local bookstore or send a self-addressed stamped envelope to:

Family Services
P.O. Box 9363
Fresno, CA 93702

Dear Reader:

We would appreciate hearing from you regarding this Harvest House book. It will enable us to continue to give you the best in Christian publishing.

1. What most influenced you to purchase *Goofy Good Clean Jokes for Kids?*
   - ☐ Author
   - ☐ Subject matter
   - ☐ Backcover copy
   - ☐ Recommendations
   - ☐ Cover/Title
   - ☐ _____

2. Where did you purchase this book?
   - ☐ Christian bookstore
   - ☐ General bookstore
   - ☐ Department store
   - ☐ Grocery store
   - ☐ Other

3. Your overall rating of this book:
   - ☐ Excellent ☐ Very good ☐ Good ☐ Fair ☐ Poor

4. How likely would you be to purchase other books by this author?
   - ☐ Very likely
   - ☐ Somewhat likely
   - ☐ Not very likely
   - ☐ Not at all

5. What types of books most interest you?
   (check all that apply)
   - ☐ Women's Books
   - ☐ Marriage Books
   - ☐ Current Issues
   - ☐ Christian Living
   - ☐ Bible Studies
   - ☐ Fiction
   - ☐ Biographies
   - ☐ Children's Books
   - ☐ Youth Books
   - ☐ Other _____

6. Please check the box next to your age group.
   - ☐ Under 18
   - ☐ 18-24
   - ☐ 25-34
   - ☐ 35-44
   - ☐ 45-54
   - ☐ 55 and over

Mail to: Editorial Director
Harvest House Publishers
1075 Arrowsmith
Eugene, OR 97402

Name _____

Address _____

City _____ State _____ Zip _____

**Thank you for helping us to help you
in future publications!**